The Mastery
of Good Luck

The Mastery of Good Luck

A MASTER CLASS COURSE WITH

Mitch Horowitz

MEDIA

Published 2019 by Gildan Media LLC
aka G&D Media
www.GandDmedia.com

THE MASTERY OF GOOD LUCK. Copyright © 2019 by Mitch Horowitz.
All rights reserved.

FIRST EDITION 2019

Interior design by Meghan Day Healey of Story Horse, LLC

Library of Congress Cataloging-in-Publication Data is available upon request

ISBN: 978-1-7225-0168-6

10   9   8   7   6   5   4   3   2   1

Contents

Introduction
The 13 Rules of Good Luck

Welcome to the Master Class Series. Each of these courses teaches you, in a series of simple, straightforward lessons, how to benefit from the powers of thought and gain a new understanding of the inner workings of life.

The lessons in this program are designed so that you may listen to one a day, all of them at once, or in whatever configuration you want. Where action steps are given, perform them in your own time and at your own pace—but it is crucial that you *do them*. This series supplies hands-on philosophy.

The Mastery of Good Luck contends that luck is not mere blind chance but rather is a network of causative factors that can be identified and cultivated. As an intriguing book called *The Kybalion* once put it: "Chance is merely a term indicating cause existing but not recognized or perceived."

This program shows you how to identify those causes and bend them to your own needs and ends. This is not a book for gamblers but for those who want to align themselves with fortune in the overall game of life.

The lesson plan consists of "13 Rules of Good Luck." In brief, the rules are:

1. Luck is learnable.
2. Good chemistry is powerfully lucky.
3. To be lucky you must be noticed.
4. Prepared minds win.
5. Sobriety is lucky.
6. Persistence beats odds.
7. Failure can be lucky.
8. "No" is not always the final answer.
9. Enthusiasm and pessimism are a lucky combination.
10. Humiliating people brings bad luck.
11. Recognizing others improves luck.
12. You must help fate find you.
13. Lucky people are decisive.

The final section, "The 13 Aphorisms of Good Luck," reviews each rule for reference.

This class, and all of the programs in the Master Class Series, is designed to provide you with a new estimate of yourself, and with the tools to fulfill your highest possibilities.

Rule
ONE

Luck Is Learnable

A neurosurgeon once told me never to take notions of luck lightly. "I've seen many patients live or die on an operating table," he said, "based on what we call luck."

Yet we have difficulty saying what luck really is. Good or bad luck could be seen merely as an accident. But is anything truly accidental when the law of cause-and-effect is detectable behind every event, even if only after the fact? Seen a certain way, we *are* able to cultivate and improve our luck. Obviously no one can control the myriad and vast factors behind every occurrence. Yet I have observed that certain practices and habits regularly improve good luck or, put another way, sway circumstances in someone's favor. This is true even if the recipient is unconscious of what's happening. Hence, the personal factors that trigger luck should always be respected, considered, and, whenever possible, cultivated.

A famous actor told a friend of mine his key to success: "Determine the things that make you lucky, and then do more of them." Implicit in his statement is the belief that certain identifiable actions, habits, personal traits, and environments are, by their nature, lucky. I not only embrace that view but I believe that many luck factors can be distilled into general rules applicable to nearly anyone's life.

I approach the topic of luck not as a statistician—although laws of odds and statistics play a part in it—but rather as a thirty-year media veteran who has observed people across a wide range of fields rise, fall, or experience inertia based on the 13 Rules explored in this program. I believe that talent and cognition matter; but I have observed, again and again, that pivotal events in people's lives, and sometimes the arc of their entire adulthoods, result from the presence or absence of the practices and disciplines you'll find here. If followed, these practices place motivated people into the current of destiny, or the flow of good luck.

Filmmaker David Lynch recalled that when he attended art school in Philadelphia he was interested in painting not in making movies. But he began to see film as a kind of "moving painting," and his interests began to shift in that direction. At a certain point he had to decide which medium to commit to. How do you know where to dedicate your energies? "Watch for those green lights," he said. Look for where you're getting the most encouragement, satisfaction, and opportunities. But, simple as it sounds, the "green lights" are not always plainly evident. Sometimes you may not feel that you're even getting any. These lessons not only help you identify the green lights but also help you position yourself in the places where they occur. This is because of the basic but neglected fact that *luck is learnable.*

Rule
TWO

Cultivate Chemistry

A person's core decision in life, observed Italian novelist Ignacio Silone, is "the choice of comrades."

The company you select plays a tremendous part not only in the values you live but also in the opportunities that you experience and the nature of what you do.

In 2010, this topic arose, albeit without full illumination, when rock legend Mick Jagger spoke to interviewer Larry King:

KING: How do you account for the longevity of the Stones as a success?

JAGGER: Well, I think the Stones are very lucky. You always need a lot of luck. And I think they were in the right place at the right time. And when we work, we work very hard. So I think you need all those things. You know, there's no good *just* being hardworking because lots of people are hardworking. But you've got to be hardworking, on your game and be lucky . . .

KING: . . . Don't eliminate the word 'luck.'

JAGGER: No, I'm not eliminating luck . . . whatever your way of life, if you get to be very successful there is usually some point where you just happen to be lucky.

One of the factors that Jagger did not mention, at least specifically, is the luck of *good chemistry*. Part of the Rolling Stones' success is that they gelled extraordinarily well as musicians, writers, performers, and in personal image and looks. They have functioned uniquely well as a group. By contrast, Jagger, a virtuoso performer and brilliant businessman, actually has a spotty record with his solo albums, despite enormous resources, fame, and talent placed behind them. His chemistry with the Rolling Stones is singular; it cannot be duplicated in other parts of his career.

Take a personal cue from this. Scan your life for areas of charmed relations and special chemistry—and preserve them. Good partnerships, whether in art, commerce, or intimate life, are rare and valuable. They are worth defending.

Years ago I had a boss whom I both loved and, at times, felt deep frustration with. I am sure he felt similarly toward me. Whenever I was tempted to leave my workplace and go it alone, I reflected on our long and extraordinary partnership, and the success it had produced. I stayed put. We possessed similar tastes, sympathies, and temperaments. Our weaknesses and strengths complemented one another's. We had a genuinely good time working together. Whatever the occasional frustrations, our joint success was truly notable. We maintained our partnership for nearly twenty years, and continue to collaborate on projects today. I view this relationship, and the chemistry inherent in it, as one of the core sources of my success.

Never take for granted the powers of relationship and collaboration. Things that you attribute to your talents alone may, in reality, be due to the intangible but vital chemistry that arises from the complementary efforts, well-balanced weaknesses and strengths, personal affinities, and shared visions that you have with a partner or workmates. Good chemistry is good luck. Seek it out. Scan your life for it. And when you find it, or if you already have, value and maintain it.

Rule
THREE

Get Noticed

You cannot profit from opportunities unless other people, including people of influence, know who you are and what you are doing. This does not mean becoming a slave to social media or a tiresome self-promoter. (Although I must grudgingly note that a not-insignificant number of self-promoters *do* meet with success.) Rather, you must honestly and plainly make clear to others your actions and enthusiasms.

A friend who works in the field of audio publishing once told me she was having difficulty getting noticed at work. She realized at a certain point that she had been concealing the enthusiasm and dedication she feels toward the projects she works on. This may have arisen from some bad advice she had received years earlier. As she told it:

I don't know why I haven't been sharing my passion at work. It may have been because years ago a manager told me that the way to get ahead in corporate publishing is to 'keep your head down.' At the time, I thought that was good, practical advice. It was not. It was a formula for mediocrity. And, most importantly, it is not me.

My friend's realization was absolutely right. The act of keeping your head down is feckless and self-defeating. And it is poor ethics: many people who keep their heads down never learn; they rarely take responsibility; and they often make others carry the load for them.

Have you ever been around someone at work who asks the same kinds of questions over and over, no matter how long they've been there? As a friend of mine put it, for such people "every day is the first day." What's really happening is that they are not listening for a meaningful answer and integrating it into their work knowledge. They are not growing. As such, they cannot be counted on. This is an unfortunate byproduct of keeping your head down.

Getting noticed and taking responsibility are far more likely, in the long run, to place you in the stream of recognition and good luck. If you step up to take responsibility there may be times when you get saddled with blame. And there may even be occasions where blame is unfairly pinned on you. But even this can be a reminder of a lucky practice: *taking credit when it is given.*

I once sat in a meeting where a publicist was complimented for scoring an important media hit. "I didn't really do anything . . ." he began to explain. A top executive turned to him and whispered: "*Take credit.* You'll get blame when you don't deserve it, too."

Be noticed. The spotlight is lucky. But it is lucky only when you are ready for it, which leads to our next lesson.

Rule
FOUR

Prepared Minds Win

In 1854 the pioneering scientist and germ theorist Louis Pasteur said in a lecture at the University of Lille in Northern France: "In the fields of observation chance favors only the prepared mind." This statement has been popularly—and, I think, accurately—shortened into: "Chance favors the prepared mind." If you wish to be lucky make this your personal motto.

Chance opportunities are useful only to those who are prepared for them—and the greater the preparation the more fully you will be able to take advantage when they arrive. Preparation heightens all of the other chance factors around you; it ensures that you'll be in the right mental state to notice, receive, and profit from opportunities.

By preparation, I do not mean using Google to peer into the lives of job interviewers or coworkers, a practice I discourage. I mean preparation of *yourself.* You should know and be reasonably versed in every aspect of your field, even as you focus on a niche or specialty within it. Be aware of current technology and developments in your field. Be well rounded about its overall practices and trends. And, above all, be an absolute expert within your area of focus. Practice your craft as a martial artist repeatedly runs a routine to the point where it becomes a part of his or her innate knowledge.

The motivational writer Dale Carnegie began his career in the early twentieth century as a teacher of public speaking. A former actor, Carnegie grasped that public speaking was becoming a vital skill for business success in the years following World War I. When preparing for a talk or pitch, Carnegie observed that you should amass so much material that you discard ninety-percent of it when actually speaking. The very fact of your preparation gives you the confidence and power to speak without notes, and to deliver a relaxing, enthusiastic, and freestyle performance.

Carnegie's formula is a recipe for good outcomes in all areas of your life. Once you are justifiably confident and expert in a task or project, you can watch, listen, intuit, and become cognizant of important cues. Ardent preparation makes you are persuasive. Your actions are natural and effortless. You can pivot. You exude confidence. You gain a childlike exuberance. And, as Pasteur alluded, things have a way of *reaching you*, or at least of reaching your attention, that would otherwise go undetected.

Preparation allows you to bend the unexpected to your advantage. Former Vermont governor and presidential candidate Howard Dean—who I once met while he was riding alone on the New York City subways—called Pasteur's expression, "chance favors the prepared mind," his personal motto. Dean repeated it to colleagues, campaign workers, and political collaborators, especially when he was chair of the Democratic National Committee. As chair, Dean insisted that the Democratic Party adopt a "50-state strategy," that is, strengthening its presence and ground operation in even those states where Democrats historically lost. If the political tide were to turn, or if a seemingly predictable race got upended, he reasoned, the more prepared party would win. This is a universally applicable principle. When opportunities appear in your path, such as a job opening, an audition, a call to present on the fly at a conference, or even being seated next to your boss or a senior manager on an air flight, the prepared person will be able to seize that golden moment. Always remember: *Luck favors the prepared mind.*

Rule
FIVE

Sobriety Is Lucky

A New York City prosecutor once told me: "If you want to avoid violence, keep away from places where large amounts of alcohol are served." He saw a repeat correlation between booze and tragic accidents or violence. A majority of cases that crossed his desk, he said, were set at clubs, sporting events, or block parties where lots of alcohol had been consumed before an argument or perceived act of disrespect escalated into physical altercation. Sometimes bystanders got hurt.

This raises a broader lesson about the personal efficacy of avoiding excess in booze or other intoxicants, and in considering staying clean altogether. It arises from a very personal story.

In the winter of 2019 I was adjusting to life after a recent divorce. One day I was gripped by a fear of financial security. Could I earn enough money, I wondered, as a writer, speaker, and narrator to make it all work? This was a serious and deeply felt question. I scanned my life for areas where I could heighten my productivity and function at the peak of my abilities. I realized, with the force of an epiphany or religious conversion, that I could take one immediate and powerful step that would invite opportunities and strengthen the good forces in my life: *stop drinking.*

In my new home environs on the glittery-grimy streets of New York's Lower East Side, I had been engaging in an increased consumption of pot, booze, and cigarettes, fueling a bit of a 1970s-style Lou Reed existence. In the back of my mind, I already knew that something had to change. Or I would. And for the worse.

A short time earlier, a close friend told me that she thought I should stop smoking. I stopped. Cold turkey. Because I knew she was right and that persisting in this habit would compromise my health and happiness. But I was unwilling to make the leap to sobriety. It seemed unnecessary. I have never had what I considered a drinking problem. I always enjoyed winding down with a drink (or a few), and also drinking at social events. I had also begun smoking pot as a near-nightly routine. Several years prior, I stopped drinking for thirty days as part of a religious commitment. And I ceased drinking for several months in fall 2009 when my first book appeared, in order to focus, nonstop, on publicity. But otherwise, I had never been clean.

That winter day in my apartment I knew that I wanted, above all, to be successful in my work. I needed to earn more. I wanted to perform at my peak. I wanted to live out my dharma. I knew that I possessed certain tools. And one that I could grasp instantly, with the greatest single payoff, was getting off booze and pot. Permanently. From past experience, I knew that sobriety would improve my energy, productivity, and sleep, as well as my proclivity to meditate and exercise.

So, I threw the junk away—literally. I told my somewhat New Age-y shrink about my intention and he counseled that I dispense with my intoxicants as part of a ceremony. I should meditate, chant, or do something to ceremonially mark my bridge into a new, clean existence. I don't actually keep any booze at home, so that was out. I thought about simply flushing my bags of weed down the toilet but that seemed anticlimactic. So, I instead took two bags of good weed, a pipe, and an old ashtray that I found on the fire escape when I moved into the place (and that I had since gotten too used to), and put them in the last of the plastic deli bags, said a prayer to my deity, and threw it all from my fifth-floor bedroom window into the courtyard-garbage area below. The ashtray hit the pavement with a booming shatter. I had been very careful that no one was there. I also went down later and dutifully cleaned it all up. I do not litter. And I felt great.

In the weeks ahead, my productivity sky-rocketed. My nights were given to work, sleep, and friends. My budget was better (booze is costly). And money flowed in.

The simplest and most impactful thing that you can do right now to heighten your abilities and avail yourself of opportunities—and to take advantage of everything that enters your path and every task and chance waiting to be maximized—is to get sober. If you need help, seek it out. It is one of the few decisions in life that is entirely in your own hands. It could change everything.

Rule
SIX

Persistence Beats Odds

I once knew a longtime editor at one of New York's largest publishing houses. In truth, he was one of the least talented people I've ever met.

His every utterance seemed predicated on consensus opinion. He conceived of (and often encumbered) book titles by stringing together lists of stock phrases. His ideas centered on copycatting whatever worked somewhere before. He gossiped, and thus alienated work-mates and colleagues. He was profoundly nervous and heightened the nerves and stress levels of people around him.

And yet for years I witnessed him survive in a fairly competitive atmosphere. Why? I believe the answer is persistence. If you stick with something long enough, and manage to avoid the swing of the thresher (and this person was lucky enough to have a fairly indulgent boss), you inevitably experience runs of good luck. And bad luck—more on which in a moment.

In the case of this person, a few of the books he published were hits just because of the odds of the wheel of life. Life is a continual ebb and flow. Consider: If a mediocre person can benefit, or at least survive, through the dice roll of chance—which in the long run includes a 50-50 average of blind luck—*imagine how much more a truly talented person stands to gain by sticking with a task.* If an uninspired person can get by in a job, how much more does a driven, meticulous, and talented person stand to gain?

If persistence possesses some hidden power, it is this: runs of luck, whether good or bad, always reverse. This is a statistical law. *And in work situations people are far more likely to recognize you for the good runs than for the bad.* One success can outweigh several failures. That may be irrational, but it is how many workplaces function. This is one of the reasons why promotions do not always appear to be based on merit.

Hence, it behooves you to stick with things. Or at least those things for which you are well suited and personally enjoy. The wheel of fortune will inevitably run your way. And the gains that you reap—especially as a prepared person—will outweigh what you will lose when the opposite occurs. In work, persistence beats the odds.

Rule
SEVEN

Failure Is Lucky

To say that "failure is lucky" isn't a cloying statement. Success guru Napoleon Hill insisted that for the motivated person failure should never be seen as final but rather as a temporary setback. I believe this is true. I can also think of numerous times in my life when a seeming failure was lucky for either one of two reasons:

1. Because it protected me from a job, course of action, or relationship for which I was unsuited, or from an environment that may have been on the perch of bad luck. I twice lost job bids and felt hurt—but the outcome was lucky. One was at a political magazine whose celebrity editor soon died in a tragic accident, plunging the magazine into disorder and failure. Another time it was to head

a publishing house that had recently been sold to a buyer who proceeded to gut and nearly wreck the place.

2. Other times failures or setbacks lit a fire within me by highlighting my own weaknesses and missteps, which actually drove me to more intelligent striving and the long-term realization of cherished aims.

Too much success, too soon, can be self-destructive. I once witnessed a talented author get catapulted to sudden notability and near-fame. Perhaps unprepared, or flawed in some deeper way, or both, his success made him insufferable to nearly everyone around him; he took advantage of his status; disrespected people and commitments; and soon grew sufficiently self-satisfied so that his work output suffered. His fame dissipated. Struggle served him better than arrival. This is true for many people.

Peaking at a young age, which is a different kind of success, can also be a disadvantage. In addition to issues of emotional preparation, this is because your run of luck arrives early, inevitably reverses, and you spend the decades ahead trying to relive past glories. At one point in my publishing career I recall noticing that nearly every writer I worked with who produced books of depth and lasting value was already in middle age. They worked all the harder—and extended their own runs of luck—because they never took their success for granted.

I want to share another personal story. I offer these not because I want to be morbidly self-disclosing but because I think I owe you an honest reckoning of how these principles have played out in my own life. When I was writing my first book *Occult America* I agreed to provide a piece of the work-in-progress as an article to a fairly small metaphysical magazine. They gratefully published it—but when the print magazine reached my home I discovered that the piece, which I felt that I provided them as a favor and which was frankly of a higher quality than their routine, was buried, more or less used as filler, and not featured on the cover.

This was in no way intended as a slight, but I nonetheless felt dejected—as though my work wasn't highly valued in the very place that it should have been. And I had also provided it for free. The episode felt like a failure. Rather than get depressed, I vowed as I held that magazine in my hands at that moment that I would not write for under-appreciative or irrelevant venues again. In the years immediately ahead my byline appeared in places including the *New*

York Times, Washington Post, Wall Street Journal, Time, Politico, and other major national media. And my articles were on the same kinds of esoteric topics I had written about up until then. I didn't compromise. That, too, was a victory.

The initial sting of poor recognition drove me to heights that I might not have otherwise reached for. What felt like a setback became a springboard to action. It was, in a sense, a *lucky failure*—from which mature victories grew.

Rule
EIGHT

"No" Is Not Always Final

A businessman and entrepreneur who I greatly admire was trying to reach out to a colleague to get together. But the colleague kept ignoring him or putting him off. Finally, they did get together—and enjoyed each other's company. My friend asked his once-hesitant companion why he had initially resisted meeting.

"Well," the other man said, "you're someone who has a reputation of not taking no for an answer." In other words, he considered my friend pushy and wasn't sure he wanted to be around him.

My friend responded pensively: "You're right. I don't take no for an answer. But it's because conditions can change, and then the answer changes."

Always remember this: *Conditions can change, and then the answer changes.*

This doesn't mean being a pest or badgering people. That will get you nowhere. It means keeping open the lines of communication and keeping relationships sound so that you can always re-approach someone. The motivational writer and essayist Elbert Hubbard wrote in his "Credo" in 1912: "I believe that when I part with you I must do it in such a way that when you see me again you will be glad—and so will I."

Don't undervalue such a sentiment. Conditions in business, and other facets of life, change or reverse all the time. This is natural law. If you have the capacity to re-approach people, and the presence of mind to do so, you can take advantage of these natural changes. So long as you've maintained positive relations, you should never feel hesitant or embarrassed about knocking on someone's door a second, third, or even fourth time. A record company executive once told me: "Be a pest, but be a nice pest."

I've personally gotten into ruts with assignment editors at magazines and newspapers only to find that after I went away for a time and then returned they became newly receptive to my pitches, possibly because of a change in the news cycle or some intangible factor that made my ideas more relevant.

I know a highly successful movie producer who has this talent for not taking no. He is unerringly friendly to nearly everyone. He offends no one and knows when to take a temporary leave. Hence, he is always ready to revisit plans, pitches, and opportunities.

When conditions shift in your favor, and someone replaces a no with a yes, accept your good luck gladly—and never remind someone of his previous refusals. You alone will know the mechanics behind the happy reversal.

Rule
NINE

Never Confuse Enthusiasm with Optimism

Philosopher Ralph Waldo Emerson famously wrote, "Nothing great was ever achieved without enthusiasm." This is true. Enthusiasm is not only infectious but it drives you to perform at your highest. Without it every task is menial.

But it is vital never to confuse enthusiasm with blind optimism. Indeed, enthusiasm coupled with a watchful wariness is a highly potent combination.

I know a lucky minority of people who continually check and recheck their work. They do so well past the point where another person would stop. Sometimes they are teased by colleagues who tell them that they ought to relax, take it slower, and not take life so seriously. Well, those who persistently recheck their work are winners. When the unexpected glitches occur they catch them before any harm is done. This has happened to me.

One summer in 2003 I was handed the dream assignment of interviewing major-league pitcher Barry Zito for the magazine *Science of Mind*. Barry used mind-metaphysics as a key part of his training routine. Landing this interview was a major "get" for the magazine, and its editors brought it to me as someone they felt they could trust with a delicate and important assignment. I was determined not to disappoint them. As it happened, the article I published, "Barry's Way," became a major springboard to my career as a writer. But it almost never occurred—and I have never written about this before. Due to a minor technical glitch, I nearly blew the entire interview. Nearly. I didn't blow it because I was wary enough to recheck my audio equipment.

The tape recorder that I was using to record my phone interview with Barry was switched to an odd function that would have entirely muted his end of the conversation. It wasn't detectable until you were recording over the phone. Had the function been left that way the whole encounter would've been lost. I had already routinely checked and tested my record function before the big event. It was fine. But I also decided, over and above what might have seemed necessary, to record a test call. When I did, I discovered the problem. It was minutes before my call with Barry. I have sometimes wondered how my life might be different today if I hadn't been healthfully paranoid enough to avert an accident, simply because I cared enough to recheck my tech details under various conditions.

It is the same with logistics, names, spellings, numbers, and arithmetic. You will never regret giving in to that creeping feeling that something may be off. Assuming the worst and rechecking your work will, at one time or another, save a huge assignment, sales presentation, legal matter, or exam I guarantee it. Let others leave early and hit the bar. You remain behind and check your work. Luck favors the pessimistic enthusiast.

Rule
TEN

Humiliate No One

It is a rule of human nature that when you insult or disrespect someone you will forget it a lot sooner than they will. In fact, when you really humiliate someone—in a meeting, online, or at a social event—that person literally never forgets. Emotions form memories. And human nature holds that most people will, at an unexpected moment, strike back if given the opportunity.

Years ago there was a politically ambitious prosecutor in New York City who aspired to one day run for mayor. She was known to belittle colleagues and subordinates. One day, she arrived late to a public meeting that began in her absence. Incensed at what she perceived as a lack of decorum, she insisted that the meeting be halted and started over in her presence. Not long after, someone leaked a story to the city tabloids about apparent excesses in her spending on office furniture. The scandal blunted her political career.

I have no idea who made the embarrassing disclosure. But I wasn't surprised to see it in headlines of a tabloid. My assumption is that her coworkers, stinging from feeling slighted, seized, either rightly or wrongly, on the opportunity to strike back. I believe the same thing happened to Minnesota Senator Amy Klobacher in the early stages of the 2020 Democratic presidential primaries. News articles ran often-anonymous accounts of how brutal a boss the candidate could be. It proved a political embarrassment.

It is not only morally wrong to wound another person's sense of self-respect, but you have no way of knowing when or whether such a score will be settled. Even if you think you can talk down to a temp or subordinate, you are wrong. That person may be privy to material that can inconvenience or embarrass you.

This same rule holds true on social media and even in supposedly private emails. You must rid yourself of the notion that anything is truly private. Confidential emails get shared all the time. And all of us have had—or will have—the experience of mistakenly hitting "reply all," or copying the wrong party, maybe even the party you're talking about. I know at least two people whose jobs were lost and lives upended, due to such innocent errors. Before you hit send, ask yourself if you've written anything that would embarrass or harm you if it got read in public. A boss once told her staff never to include anything in an email that you wouldn't want read aloud in a court of law with you on the witness stand.

When you're posting on social media, the temptation to be snarky and sarcastic can be nearly irresistible. People feel disinhibited by distance or anonymity, and tones of irony and sarcasm tend to be the general mode of online communication. Always rememeber that online comments are forever, even when erased. Anonymity may afford some protection but I have my doubts. And, believe me, when you insult someone online that person remembers it—always. They may circle back at an unexpected moment. And if you do flame someone or wound their feelings, whether online, at work, or in public, sometimes in a moment of anger or stress, then apologize. And do so sincerely.

My one basic rule is that you shouldn't post anything that you wouldn't be willing to say to someone's face. Another, even blunter rule will rescue you in advance from the misfortune of trash-talking or online feuds. An entrepreneur said it to me, and I've never forgotten it: "Next time you have the opportunity to be a smartass—don't." It could save your job and your peace of mind.

Rule
ELEVEN

Recognize Others

This rule builds on the one we just considered about not humiliating people. Rather than merely avoiding offense, you should actively build people up, sincerely and when it is properly due. Get in the habit of thanking people and recognizing their contribution to a project, and do so in cold, hard cash when the occasion calls for it.

Saying thank you is not just a matter of courtesy and ethics, although it is both. By recognizing other people, both privately and publicly, you allow them to feel that they benefit from your success, and you give them a stake in its continuance.

Philosopher William James observed in 1896: "The deepest principle of Human Nature is the craving to be appreciated." People hunger to be seen. Never underestimate the power of simple recognition. It is usually free, and it brings with it immense and unseen value. Those who feel that you have recognized them will endeavor to find a lost or late check, to put you first on a list, and to make sure your package goes out after the office closes.

The opposite also holds true. If you fail to recognize people they won't necessarily hinder your work, but they will feel apathy toward your needs. I have been thanked innumerable times, and I have truly appreciated it. But, in full disclosure, I must confess that I more keenly recall the times when I have not been appropriately thanked. Perhaps you do, too. It is a fissure in human nature that we are more likely to recall expectations unfulfilled than fulfilled. I don't know why—it might have to do with some primal need for safety. In any case, it should always be remembered that "invisible helpers" appear based on whether we have thanked and recognized them. Recognizing people is homage to the gods of luck.

In matters of money, you can and should remunerate valuable people. But even if you cannot do so, or have reasons for not doing so, you can accrue similar benefit by *paying them quickly*. I cannot fully emphasize the goodwill engendered when you pay a contractor, employee, or helper quickly—preferably on completion of the task. That is how you pay a barber or stylist. Why not a contract worker? Quick pay often means as much or more than the sum itself. I know a publisher who pays people by electronic transfer in 24 to 48 hours after delivery of a project. It breeds tremendous loyalty. It is also good ethics. By contrast, I know firsthand of educational and spiritual centers that drag their feet on paying even modest sums to speakers and workshop facilitators. I cannot speak for others, but I will never work for such places again. You value someone's work not only in cash but also in how you tender it. Speed is free. Its dividends are invaluable.

Rule
TWELVE

Show Up

Are you reliable? A large part of what makes someone reliable is the simple but vital act of showing up, and showing up on time, for his or her commitments, social and work-related. You have no idea how fully other people notice this and judge you by it. What's more, reliably showing up puts you into the flow of luck.

In today's culture, people feel too at ease bailing on commitments, whether family, social or work-related, for just about any reason. The need to run an errand is not a sufficient excuse. Busyness is not a sufficient excuse (at least usually). Nor is feeling a bit under-the-weather or having a cold. We as a culture are, I believe, too self-coddling. We deem things as urgent that are merely passing. As a philosopher friend of mine put it: "The only real emergency is a medical emergency."

Keeping your engagements and commitments not only marks you for reliability but it does more. Important and often fortuitous things happen to those who place themselves in the flow of life. Chance encounters, of the most unexpected variety, can open you to a new job or give you the break for which you are searching. I am not suggesting that you should go to every engagement with the anxious expectation that you'll meet someone vital—but the odds are that one day it will occur.

One night a close friend was hosting a party. I was in attendance but I felt bored and out of sorts. I was going to skip out early. But then I thought: no, out of loyalty to my friend, who wanted me there, I should stick around. A woman showed up about forty-five minutes later who became my future wife. We had two children together. This is how strangely life works. If I had left, and let down my friend, I would not have met a vital, central person in my life. I wasn't sticking around for personal gain. I was doing it to honor my friend. But the very fact of feeling an obligation to another, and thus remaining in the flow of life, placed me in the path of a positive, life-changing experience.

I know a woman who was supposed to attend a friend's book reading one night. She begged off because she had a minor cold. The writer was disappointed. It colored his perception of his friend as someone unwilling to go the distance for him. I have often wondered what good thing might have happened had she showed up that night. Possibly nothing. Possibly something life-changing. We will never know. But it is clear to me that fate shines on those it can reach. And that means those who show up.

Here is a story of a slightly different tenor. It may seem extreme but consider it carefully. One night I was speaking with a group of successful photographers. These were people who had distinguished themselves in the hard-knuckled world of photojournalism. It happened that many of them had known each other when they were younger and working as interns at *Time* magazine in New York. As the night went on, they started trading "war stories." To laughter all around, one of them recounted a time when he was tasked with bringing important film from a news assignment across town to the magazine's offices. On the way he got into a car accident, which, thankfully, wasn't grave but was serious enough so that an ambulance was called and paramedics removed him from his car.

Asked how he was feeling, he started saying in halting terms that he needed to get this film across town. The group of photographers laughed at what had seemed an absurd mis-match of priorities. The speaker himself was good-natured about it and, since no one was hurt, it *was* the kind of story that one could look back on and laugh. But consider how few people would demonstrate the kind of instinc-tive dedication he displayed that day when he thought only of completing his assignment. (And the film did get there.) Certainly you could say that it was going too far, or that he dis-played an unhealthy degree of one-sidedness. But is that really so? Wouldn't you want your surgeon, nurse, pilot, caregiver, or someone in law enforcement to demonstrate that kind of dedication? Yes, the example is perhaps extreme. But it highlights the character of peo-ple who distinguish themselves—and who get places. Every successful photographer who sat in on our discussion that night had a similar attitude or story. Learn from it.

Rule
THIRTEEN

Act Quickly

Decisiveness is a key element in good luck. Opportunity comes and goes quickly. It does not linger. "Time dissipates energy," a powerful agent once told me. When you are presented with a good chance—move on it. Slowness either dampens or negates opportunities.

Quick and decisive action should not be confused with impulsiveness. If you are following all of the other rules laid out here you will not fall victim to blind impulse. You will have sufficient information about yourself and your surroundings, and sufficient preparation, so that you will be able to move smartly and quickly when the wheel of fortune stops where you are standing. Intuition arises from amassing and storing a huge amount of information so that when chance arrives the prepared person has "data banks" on which to rely.

Fortune hits you with speed. I know a brilliant singer-songwriter who had top-ten hits in the 1990s. She told me that when fame came her way "it all happened so quickly." As a skilled performer and artist, she was ready. Not everything went smoothly, of course. But she sailed to the top of the charts with her vision and integrity intact.

When people are searching for a job or a breakthrough in life I always remind them that no matter how many opportunities seem to slip through their fingers "it only takes one yes." Be on the lookout for that one yes, and be ready to seize it. It doesn't matter what transpired before it and how many heartaches preceded it. They will all be forgotten once it comes.

A philosopher once asked me: "What do you do when someone offers you a gift?" I looked back at him blankly. "You accept it!" he replied. This is exactly what life is like in all of its facets: When something good comes your way—an offer, a job, an opportunity—do not dither. You will recognize it as an opportunity because of everything we've been covering up to this point.

And if it's the wrong opportunity you can handle it with a quick no. But the unluckiest thing you can do, and a harbinger of troubles to come, is to demonstrate half-heartedness, delay, or silence. No employer or backer worth having will respect that. He or she wants to know that your dedication matches his own. Life permits no halfway measures. When chances reach you, act on them.

Appendix

The 13 Aphorisms of Good Luck

1. Good luck is not a synonym for happy chance. It is more often a selection of habits and personal techniques that can be cultivated to maximize events that enter your life. Luck is learnable.

2. Be on the watch for fruitful collaborations. Valuable chemistry is irreplaceable. In areas of your life where it already exists, honor it, cultivate it, and maintain it. Chemistry is the root and product of good luck.

3. Luck comes to those who are seen. Act with dignity and decorum but ensure that people are aware of your work, your passions, and your contributions.

4. Luck favors the prepared mind. You can only take advantage of chances when you are able to use them. Preparation invites chances. The prepared eye notices things no one else does.

5. The decision to quit drinking and drugs is one of the most powerful you can ever make. It can increase your effectiveness, output, and opportunities in all areas of life. It is one of the few major decisions placed wholly in your own hands.

6. It is a statistical law that runs of luck always reverse. A fertile period replaces a fallow one. And back again. In workplaces successes are often remembered more than failures. This is why persistence beats the odds.

7. Failure or setbacks can rescue you from contact with the wrong people and circumstances. They can also rouse you to work better and stronger, and to aim higher. For the luck-oriented person, failure can be a springboard.

8. A successful person once said: "Conditions can change, and then the answer changes." Hence, you should make a practice of revisiting missed possibilities—and keep-

ing your relations positive so that you can revisit them.

9. Never confuse enthusiasm with optimism. Check and recheck your work. Watch constantly for errors. You will find them. Mishaps will be averted. Entire projects are saved by pessimistic enthusiasm.

10. Any time you humiliate someone you run the risk of laying a hidden time bomb somewhere on your path. People rarely forget, and sometimes avenge, humiliations.

11. Thanking and recognizing people—publicly, privately, and sometimes financially—helps them feel a shared stake in your project. They may come to your aid at subtle and important moments. Neglecting to do so invites others to feel apathy (if not antipathy) toward your needs.

12. Fate shines only on those it can reach. Show up. Keep commitments. Be in the flow of life.

13. Opportunities don't linger. When they arrive you must act quickly and decisively. If you are prepared, this isn't impulsivity. Decisiveness is intelligent and luck inducing.

About the Author

Mitch Horowitz is a PEN Award-winning historian and the author of books including *Occult America; One Simple Idea: How Positive Thinking Reshaped Modern Life;* and *The Miracle Club: How Thoughts Become Reality.* A lecturer-in-residence at the University of Philosophical Research in Los Angeles, Mitch introduces and edits G&D Media's line of Condensed Classics and is the author of the Napoleon Hill Success Course series, including *The Miracle of a Definite Chief Aim* and *The Power of the Master Mind.* His other titles in the Master Class Series include: *The Science of Getting Rich Action Plan; Miracle: The Ideas of Neville Goddard;* and *Awakened Mind: How Thoughts Create Reality.* Visit him at MitchHorowitz.com.